Humor
And Other Life Seasonings

Humor
And Other Life Seasonings

Cathy Burnham Martin

Published and printed in the United States of America

QUIET
THUNDER

www.QTPublishing.com

Quiet Thunder Publishing

Naples, FL   Manchester, NH   Columbus, NC

This title and more can be found at
www.GoodLiving123.com

Paperback edition: ISBN 978-1-939220-75-2
eBook edition: ISBN 978-1-939220-76-9
Audiobook edition: ISBN 978-1-939220-77-6

Library of Congress Control Number: 2025920852

Dedication

"Humor" is gleefully dedicated to everyone who has made me laugh. And I love to laugh. Thank you for encouraging great glee.

Studies show that children laugh between 300 and 400 times every day. By the time we are adults, we laugh only 15-20 times daily. Okay. Life gets more serious with lots more responsibilities as we age, but laughter is healthy for us at all ages.

Bravo to the comedians, writers, and other performers who did not let growing older mean inhibiting their sense of humor. We need to celebrate spontaneity and appreciate the lighter side of life.

Thank you for putting a smile on my face. Bless you for keeping laughter in our lives.

Cathy

(Photo by Mikael Kristenson)

Foreword

How would we survive without humor? I truly don't know. I think we all tend to take ourselves too seriously much of the time. I strive to take what I do seriously, but I accept that I am a mere human, filled with faux pas.

What do you call a faux pas at a fondue party?
A fondon't.

Some of my favorite moments in life have been filled with humor's happiness. Sometimes we laugh out loud. Other times a chuckle is garnered. Still other times, we crack a wry smile.

If we had memorable teachers during our lives, chances are good that they knew how to use humor. This powerful educational skill creates better attention in students and reflects an effective ability to engage with students of all ages, but especially children.

Teacher joke: *Q: Why wouldn't the elephant use the computer?*
A: He was afraid of the mouse.

Perhaps we all like to think we are funny, and we probably are from time to time. Most of us likely overrate how funny we think we are. That doesn't mean we should stop trying. The more we pay attention to the recipient, rather than ourselves, the wittier we can seem.

(Photo by Braydon Anderson)

"Honey, I'm not always funny,
but I'm always honest.
And sometimes,
honesty is the funniest thing of all."

-- Carol Burnett (1933 -)
American comedian, actress, & singer

"*A person who knows how to laugh at himself will never cease to be amused.*"
— Shirley MacLaine (1934 -)
American actress, dancer & author

(Photo by Shubham Dhage)

"We don't laugh because we're happy – we're happy because we laugh."

– William James (1842 – 1910)
American philosopher & psychologist

(Photo by Getty Images)

Table of Contents

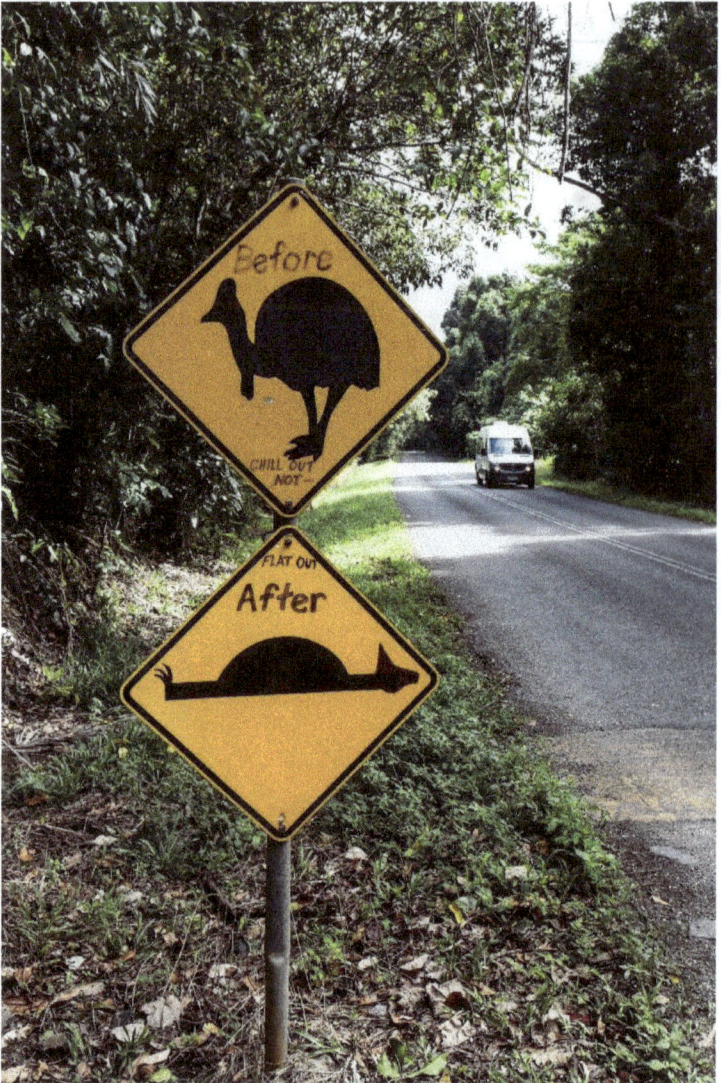

(Photo by David Clode)

Laughter

Chuckle or chortle, giggle or guttural, infectious or ironical, laughter is beyond the very best medicine. Whether our laugh is high-pitched, maniacally triumphant, subtly sarcastic, or an unrestrained cachinnation, laughter is marvelous.

Think of a laugh as both personal and situational. We can utter a sweet little laugh or throw our heads back in great glee. Precious are the moments when we get to enjoy the very best, which must be the whole-hearted belly laugh.

(Photo by Denis Agati)

Psychologists tend to separate humor into types or groups. Some will refer to three primary types. Superiority humor is typically the best, making an audience or receiver of the comedy feel superior as the humorist uses self-deprecating humor.

*"I got in a fight one time
with a really big guy,
and he said, 'I'm going to
mop the floor with your face.'
I said, 'You'll be sorry.'
He said, 'Oh, year? Why?'
I said, 'Well, you won't be able to
get into the corners very well."*

-- Emo Phillips (1956 -)
American stand-up comedian
(Noted for using paraprosdokians, or funny,
unexpected ending twists)

Psychologists also refer to the scripted humor of incongruity. This is where we may see puns, satire or a juxtaposition between what is and what should be.

A good example might be the Gary Larson "Far Side" comic strip. Even easier to see are the modern elements amidst the Stone Age setting of "The Flintstones."

*"I'm quite a compulsive person, but I'm also very indecisive.
I don't know what I want, but I know that I want it now."*

-- Dylan Moran (1971 -)
Irish comedian, writer & actor

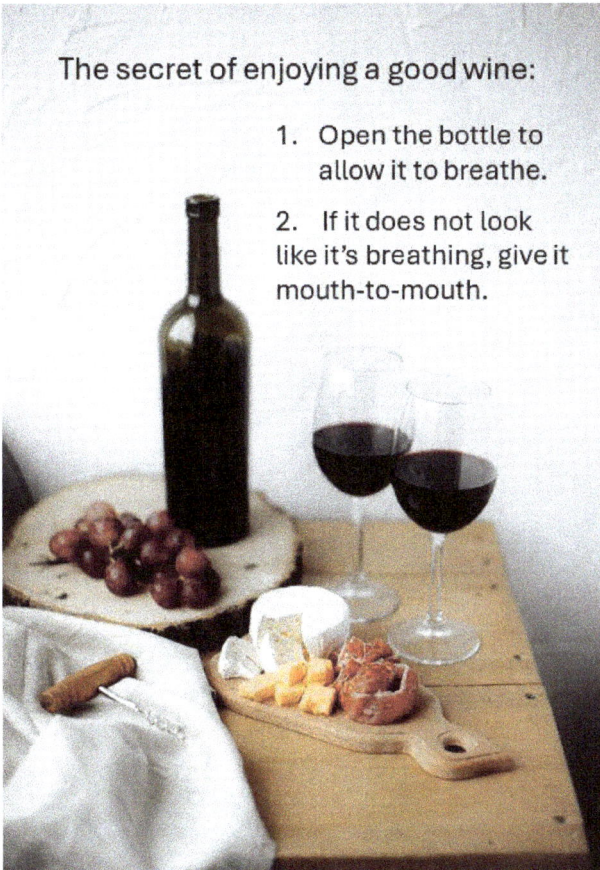

The secret of enjoying a good wine:

1. Open the bottle to allow it to breathe.

2. If it does not look like it's breathing, give it mouth-to-mouth.

(Photo by Kateryna Hliznitsova)

The third major area is called relief. Humor of this type delivers a punchline that relieves a tension that has been created. We often see this style in a hero's sidekick.

Frantic patient: *"Doctor, I keep thinking I'm a pair of curtains!"*
Doctor: *"Pull yourself together."*
(Ahhhhh, metaphor.)

Other experts divide types of humor up into areas like physical, emotional, cognitive, and social. However we choose to categorize humor, we'll look at lots of variations and how they make us laugh.

(Photo by Charles DeLuvio)

"My psychiatrist told me I was crazy, and I said, 'I want a second opinion.'
He said, 'Okay. You're ugly, too.'"

-- Rodney Dangerfield (1921 - 2004)
American stand-up comedian & actor

Humor is not just enjoyable. It plays a vital role in our lives and boosts our overall well-being. Laughter makes us healthier physically, mentally, and socially.

Laughter is a powerful strategy to support mental health. Humor reduces stress and anxiety by decreasing stress hormones like cortisol, which helps us relax.

Humor is a welcome distraction from worries and problems. It gives us a temporary escape from negative emotions.

It boosts our mood and positive outlook. Laughing releases endorphins and other neurochemicals like dopamine and serotonin. Humor promotes feelings of joy and happiness.

Comedy helps us cope and become more resilient. It lets us reframe difficult scenarios and see them from a less negative perspective.

*"Laughter gives us distance.
It allows us to step back from an event,
deal with it and then move on."*

-- Bob Newhart (1929 – 2024)
American comedian & actor

(Photo by Chaitanya Pillala)

Well-balanced people often use light-heartedness to cope positively with stress and difficult times. Studies suggest that laughter can not only alleviate but reverse our body's stress response.

A good sense of humor is seen as a positive psychological strength. It helps us develop strength and messages of hope in the face of adversity. With humor we can help others feel good and build their resilience to stress.

Humor is a great avenue through which we can express emotions. This can be especially helpful following or even during pain, sorrows, or other difficulties. Because it releases endorphins, humor can temporarily reduce pain and increase pain tolerance. In fact, studies have shown that laughter can be as much as 500 times more effective than morphine at eliminating physical pain.

*"Always laugh when you can.
It is cheap medicine."*

-- Lord Byron (George Gordon Byron)
(1788 – 1824)
English poet

Laughter improves our cardiovascular health by increasing our heart rate and blood flow. Mayo Clinic studies have shown that finding moments of joy and humor helps us stay healthy by lowering our blood pressure and promoting smooth blood flow.

"Be careful about reading health books. You may die of a misprint."

-- Mark Twain (1835 – 1910)
American writer & humorist

Now, consider this. Laughter burns calories. This is especially true of hearty laughter. Making our abdominal muscles work contributes to burning calories, albeit modestly. Hearty laughter also helps relieve physical tension by relaxing our muscles.

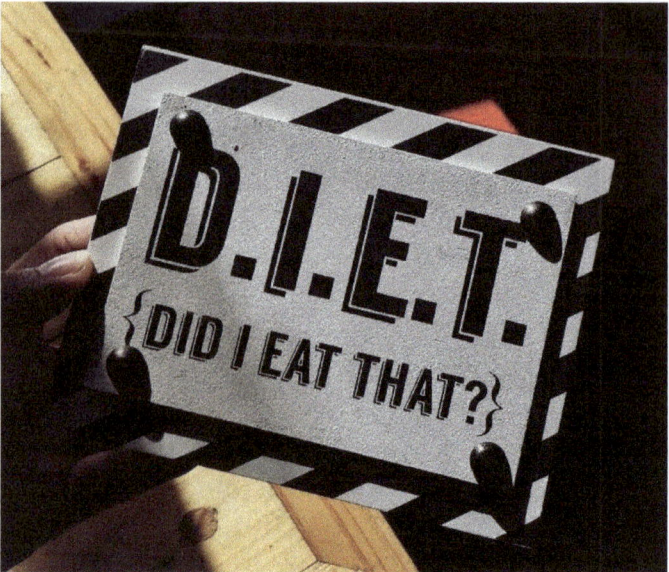

(Photo by Jarnie Matocinos)

Humor helps relieve depression, anxiety and even insomnia. It not only makes it easier to fall asleep, but lets us enjoy a more restful sleep, thus improving sleep quality.

When selecting a television program or movie to watch before bedtime, we often choose dramas. However, laughter is highly useful in promoting better sleep. So, a silly or clever comedy would be a far better choice.

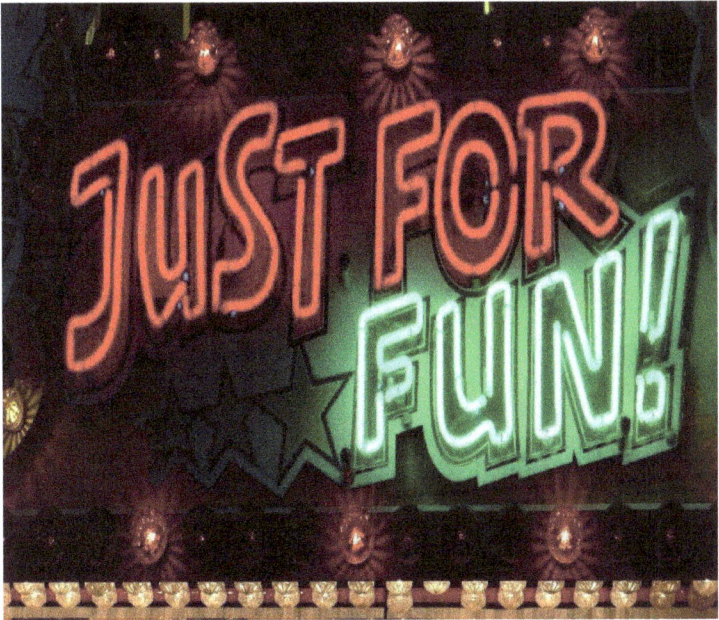

Laughter is just plain important, especially after all the social isolation we all likely experienced during the Covid-19 lockdowns. In truth, laughing enhances our immune function by increasing the number of immune cells and infection-fighting antibodies.

"Everybody laughs the same in every language because laughter is a universal connection."

-- Jakov Smirnoff (stage name of Yakov Naumovich Pokhis) (1951 -)
Soviet American comedian, actor & writer

(Photo by Victoria Romulo)

2

Social Function

"Laughter is the shortest distance between two people."

-- Victor Borge (1909 – 2000)
Danish American actor, comedian & pianist

Humor helps us bring people together and foster common bonds that strengthen relationships. The ability to use well-placed witty remarks is more than a personality trait. We think of it as a strong quality or a treasured ability when someone can be amusing or comical.

When we think of someone as humorous, we are noting their genuine sense of fun. Funny people see and express the comic, humorous version of an incident. Sometimes they simply seem to have a pleasantly funny view of life.

"People say that money is not the key to happiness, but I always figured if you have enough money, you can have a key made."

-- Joan Rivers (1933 – 2014)
American comedian, actress, producer & writer

Humor can help with conflict resolution and tension reduction in business and personal relationships. It does this by diffusing tense situations, softening disagreements, and facilitating more constructive conversations by reducing anger and resentment.

Laughter helps us communicate more openly and freely. This is especially helpful when discussing sensitive topics. Humor reflects a positive mood or state of mind, both of which are helpful in successful communications.

"I've noticed that everyone who is for abortion has already been born."

-- Ronald Reagan (1911 – 2004)
American actor & politician
40th President of the United States

Some of the most effective advertising campaigns are based on humor, because humor helps our content be more memorable and likeable. Of course, bad attempts at humor become tedious to the viewer, inspiring us to change the channel.

Humorous people are often seen as more attractive. We like wit. We find funny people to be more engaging and socially attractive.

Sharing laughter plays a powerful role in building stronger relationships and connections. It fosters emotional bonds and increases our feelings of closeness. It brings people together with a sense of fellowship, happiness, and well-being.

A good sense of humor is high on lists of strong leadership skills. Laughter, when not at the expense of others, helps us get along with people and helps make conversations memorable.

Humor breaks down barriers and creates more open environments in various relationships, be they professional, familial, or romantic. Close friends, partners, and spouses tend to laugh at many of the same things. Laughter connects us culturally and lets us comment on societal issues, from politics to family norms.

(Photo by Jamie Haughton)

In romantic comedy we enjoy watching love and laughter grow along with relationships. Sometimes stories are screwball, sometimes satirical, and sometimes traditional.

Think about movies like 1989's "When Harry Met Sally." The romantic comedy battle of the sexes follows bumpy roads but delivers a happy ending, while making us laugh and sometimes cry in the process. Hmmmm… much like real life.

Other twists in romantic comedy may involve disguises or masquerade. A memorable example is found in the 1959 film "Some Like It Hot," starring Marilyn Monroe, Tony Curtis, and Jack Lemmon. While we have fun watching, it's clear they also had fun making the movie. Humor doesn't get much better than that.

(Photo by David Clode)

3

High-Brow/Low-Brow

We find strong emotional connections in comedy, from base humor to empathy. Laughter helps us connect through personal stories.

High-brow humor is not humor for snobs. However, it does inspire or require our minds to think and delve into layers of thoughts. Think of comedians and writers who play with words and meanings. Double meanings, known as double entendre, reflects high-brow humor.

Here's an example. You stare thoughtfully into the distance and say, *'You know, a really deep analogy is like a cloud.'* Your interlocuter seems confused. You suddenly snap back into the moment and give an apologetic, *'Oh, I'm sorry. That was over your head.'*

Or, here is another example:

Lady Nancy Astor: *"Winston, if you were my husband, I'd poison your tea."*

Winston: *"Nancy, if I were your husband, I'd drink it."*

We typically experience what can be called low-brow humor. This reflects lines and jokes designed simply to create laughter and can appeal to our silly sense.

Low-brow comedy includes boisterous jokes or even scolding an audience. Don Rickles, also known as "The Merchant of Venom" and "Mr. Warmth," was famous for this.

"I wouldn't insult you, but then again, you're not bright enough to notice."

-- Don Rickles (1926 – 2017)
American stand-up comedian & actor

(Photo by Michel Grolet)

Another low-brow example is found in a comedian behaving as if utterly drunk. Foster Brooks is best known for his lovable drunk act, complete with plenty of belching.

"Flying up there with those big fluffy things.
(Burrrrp!)
Clouds? Oh, are you a pilot too?"

-- Foster Brooks (1912 – 2001)
American comedian & actor

(Photo by Hussain Badshah)

Low-brow humor includes toilet humor, fart jokes, or silliness often referred to as sophomoric.

(Photo by Getty Images)

*"Whomever said
laughter is the best medicine
clearly hasn't tried curing diarrhea
with a tickle fight."*

-- Anonymous

Some comedians deliver performances that can fall into both categories. Think of observational humor, for example.

It can be base and off-the-cuff or spring from deeper thoughts. Verbal humor can easily land in both high-brow and low-brow arenas.

If you remember the 1960s-70s television show "Laugh-In" and movies such as 2005's "Wedding Crashers", for example, you recall a distinctly popular, low-brow comedy program. On the other hand, films by Woody Allen could be low-brow or high-brow or combine both in one film.

> *"I'm not afraid of death; I just don't want to be there when it happens."*
>
> -- Woody Allen (1935 -)
> American filmmaker, actor & comedian

(Photo by Diane Alkier)

1971's "Bananas", 1972's "Everything You Always Wanted to Know about Sex", 1973's "Sleeper" and 1982's "A Midsummer Night's Sex Comedy" are liltingly low-brow. 1977's "Annie Hall" and 1978's "Interiors" are distinctly high-brow. Audiences must read between the lines, so to speak, as there is no attempt at base humor.

(Photo by Frank Tokluoglu)

4

Observation

The best comedians are superb storytellers. They project high (or deliberately low) energy, appropriate tone, and perfect pacing to reach each scenario's conclusion. And they leave their audience wanting more, naturally.

Jay Leno is rightly noted as a king of observation. He built his comedic kingdom by being relatable and helping us laugh at our silly selves.

I found him to be down to earth and quick-witted, both great traits for a comedian. Following one interview I did with him for television news, he asked if he could borrow my microphone. He proceeded to look into the camera lens and deliver a promo for that night's story.

Of course, Leno quipped, *"Good evening. I'm Cathy Burnham after a major operation."* Then he did a retake replacing the operation line with *"Look a little different? Coming up tonight at 11, I'll have an interview with my friend, Jay Leno."*

Naturally, I opted to use *his* promo and not my own. Viewers loved it!

Jerry Seinfeld is a great example of observational anecdotes. He built a solid career as New York's "man-on-the-street." His observation skills turn everyday occurrences into humor. He has studied our human quirks and finds the funny side.

"A bookstore is one of the only pieces of evidence we have that people are still thinking."

-- Jerry Seinfeld (1954 -)
American comedian & actor

(Photo by Ashley Byrd)

"I think it's funny to be delicate with subjects that are explosive."

-- Jerry Seinfeld (1954 -)
American comedian & actor

(Photo by Leo Visions)

"Sometimes the road less traveled is less traveled for a reason."

-- Jerry Seinfeld (1954 -)
American comedian & actor

"I read that the number one fear of the average person is [public] speaking.
Number two was death.
To me, that means that, to the average person,
if you were going to be at a funeral,
you would rather be in the casket
than doing the eulogy."

-- Jerry Seinfeld (1954 -)
American comedian & actor

Observational storytelling is characterized by long monologues or narratives. These focus on social interests or human behavior.

These humorists have a particular knack for finding merry madness in the mundane. Anecdotal comedy turns our own personal stories, whether real or exaggerated, into delightful humor.

"Get your facts first;
then you can distort them as you please."

-- Mark Twain (1835 – 1910)
American writer & humorist

The ability to see humor in daily life has also created comedic journalism. Smart, sassy comedians and writers manage to find the comic tone in hot news, translating it to audiences with wit and satire. Greg Gutfeld is a superb example of comedic media/journalism. He states facts about virtually any serious topic of the day and quickly takes a more subjective stance without offending audiences. Well, if his studio audience groans or reacts oddly, the comedian in him instantly lets his arsenal of funny faces soften the blow.

"If America oppresses, why do so many people risk their lives coming here to be oppressed?"

-- Greg Gutfeld (1964 -)
American TV host, political commentator,
comedian & author

(Photo by Fabian Fauth)

Though not neutral, comedic journalists are often more trusted than traditional journalistic media types because they make a positive emotional connection with their viewers. We like people who make us think and laugh. We are not drawn to people who yell at us or put down our beliefs.

"Thomas Jefferson once said, 'We should never judge a president by his age, only by his works.' And ever since he told me that, I stopped worrying."

-- Ronald Reagan (1911 – 2004)
American actor & politician
40th President of the United States

(Photo from Library of Congress)

A clever storytelling humorist captures our attention and our imagination. These are intellectuals who use humor or wit in writing and public speaking.

Unlike comedians, they are not solely seeking laughs, although they often get them. When we think of sage witticisms and strong storytellers who use humor, names like Mark Twain, Noel Coward, Will Rogers, and Neil Simon come to mind.

"It's better to keep your mouth closed and let people think you are a fool than to open it and remove all doubt."

-- Mark Twain (1835 – 1910)
American writer & humorist

(Photo by David Clode)

5

Physical

The joys of physical humor have long been treasured in the form of mimes, clowns, and slapstick comedy. Stunts and visual gags form the oldest type of humor, originating from the Italian "commedia dell'arte."

(Photo by Christo Anestev)

"Hello, I'd like to register for mime classes."
"Ah, say no more."

Magnificent mimes like Charlie Chaplin, Buster Keaton, and Marcel Marceau made physical humor a comedy standard. The style is classic in silent films and vaudeville, filled with silly sight gags, exaggerated body language, and unnatural speed, be it frantically fast or soooo slow.

- - - - -

A mime is working at a zoo. One day, the head zookeeper pulls him aside to chat. He says, *'Bobo, our silverback gorilla, the star attraction here at the zoo, has died. We don't want to lose the revenue, so we want to hire you to dress up in a gorilla suit and pretend to be bobo. We'll pay you triple what you're making now.'*

The mime agrees and starts the next day. At first, it's fine, and he enjoys being Bobo. But after a couple of weeks of doing the same thing every day he's a bit bored. So, he decides to give the audience a real show. He climbs to the very top of his enclosure and swings around, pounding his chest. The crowd is loving it. Just then, he slips and topples over the fence into the next enclosure, which is the lion's pen.

The lion starts to go after him, and at first the mime keeps up the shtick, running away like a gorilla. But as the lion gets closer he gives up and just runs as fast as he can.

Finally, the lion leaps on him and pins him down. Now he gives up on the whole bit and starts yelling, *'Help! Hel'! I'm a person in here! Call the zookeepers! HELP!!!!!'*

And the lion goes, *'Dude, you're gonna get us both fired.'*

- - - - -

(Photo by Dan Cook)

Of course, visual humor is not necessarily silent. Comedy series including "The Three Stooges," cartoons like "The Roadrunner," and movies like "Naked Gun" took absurdity and physical gags to new levels.

(Photo from Looney Tunes Wiki Fandom)

Today we think of it as the trips, slips, and doubletakes of broad humor. Dick van Dyke comes to mind, stumbling into the opening credits of his weekly television show. The famed series "Gilligan's Island" capitalized on physical humor and absurd situations. Actor Jim Carrey's body language and wildly exaggerated facial expressions epitomize physical humor.

6

Verbal

Sometimes we hear a mild or indirect word or expression substituted for another that is considered to be too harsh or blunt. Such euphemisms are intended to amuse or downplay something unpleasant or embarrassing.

These are not to be confused with pithy observations that contain general truths that have been misquoted or construed out of context. Aphorisms are frequently used as a source of humor.

> *"Humor is reason gone mad."*
>
> -- Groucho Marx (1890 – 1977)
> American comedian, actor & writer

Juxtaposition is also popular as humor uses two things that are seemingly contradictory or unlikely. This paradoxical playing typically finds confusion between two characters or cases of mistaken identity. That is a popular Shakespearean theme. Consider the foolery of "The Comedy of Errors" in which confusion abounds thanks to two sets of twins.

Wordplay with our language has long been a vibrant part of humor. Double entendre and funny phrase twists make our minds dance.

Verbal humor can be low-brow as with television shows such as "Rowan & Martin's Laugh-In" that launched its six-season run in 1968. It can be silly and sassy as with the American humor "Mad" magazine that launched in 1952.

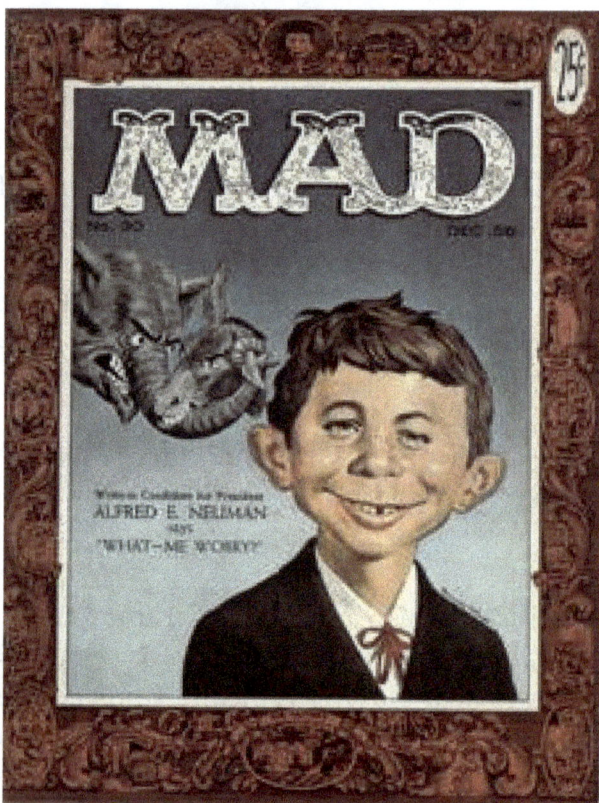

(*Mad 30* – published December, 1956)

The element of surprise breathes fabulous life into comedy. We love falling for clever and quick humor with unexpected twists or punchlines.

It takes great intelligence and quick wit to form the funny phrases that make audiences howl, also in a happy high-brow fashion. My favorite example of this skill comes from Richard Lederer. This all-time great American linguist is noted for his books on the English language.

One day, I enjoyed the distinct honor of interviewing him for a 30-minute, live studio audience television program. It mattered not what questions I asked. Lederer's rapid-fire responses sparkled almost as brilliantly as the constant twinkle in his eye. He deftly wove his arsenal of puns, oxymorons and anagrams into each response. Utterly brilliant.

I was humbled and honored when the best-selling author of "Anguished English" and other books about language and humor reviewed my 2017 book, "The Bimbo Has Brains: And Other Freaky Facts." Richard Lederer said, *"The Bimbo Has Brains... and insight and compassion and empathy and outreach and bubbling-over humor. Cathy Burnham Martin's book is so human and so immensely caring that it will change lives."* Thank you again, Richard!

(Photo from San Diego Oasis)

"English is a crazy language. There is no egg in eggplant nor ham in hamburger; neither apple nor pine in pineapple. English muffins weren't invented in England or French fries in France… We take English for granted.
But if we explore its paradoxes, we find that quicksand can work slowly, boxing rings are square, and a guinea pig is neither from Guinea nor is it a pig."

-- Richard Lederer (1938 -)
American linguist, speaker, academic & author

Whether reading, watching or listening to a punster or other talented linguist, enjoy verbal humor whenever possible. Twisting language, witticisms, ironic statements, slang, rhymes, tongue-in-cheek statements, acronyms, alliteration, onomatopoeia, and more keep our brains active and alert, while bringing laughter to our lips.

While discussing verbal humor, we must remember to include Dad jokes. This is the nickname given to all those unoriginal or unfunny jokes that have been supposedly (or actually) told by middle-aged or older men. Think of these as the anti-humor jokes that elicit groans from the audience. These are often puns or one-liners.

What do you call someone
who tells Dad jokes but isn't a Dad?
A faux pa.

Here's a Dad joke example. Dad explains that Fred Flintstone would yell, *"Yabba daba doooo!"* at the start of every episode. He continues, *"The people in Dubai don't like 'The Flintstones,' but the people in Abu Dhabi do."*

Then everyone groans, *"Oh, Dad!"*

"Wait! I have another one! What does a French Fred Flintstone say when he arrives?"

No one answers, but Dad is ready with the response. *"Yabba dabb-adieu!"* More groans.

7

Parody Plus

"Parody is satire without the fangs."

-- Richard Raymond III (1932 -)
American author & former US Marine officer

Some humor uses imitation or mockery for comedy. These include horseplay, buffoonery, and crude characterizations. Often parodies feature ludicrously impossible situations that stretch way beyond simple silliness. Farcical approaches reflect deliberate exaggerations or spoofs, poking fun at something serious or using comedy to pay tribute.

Think of the 1987 Mel Brooks movie "Spaceballs." Dark Helmet replaced Darth Vadar. *"May the Schwartz be with you"* replaced *"May the force be with you."* Princess Vespa parodied Princess Leia.

While primarily parodying the "Star Wars" trilogy, other films got a few loving jabs, too. These included "The Wizard of Oz," "Star Trek," and even "Planet of the Apes."

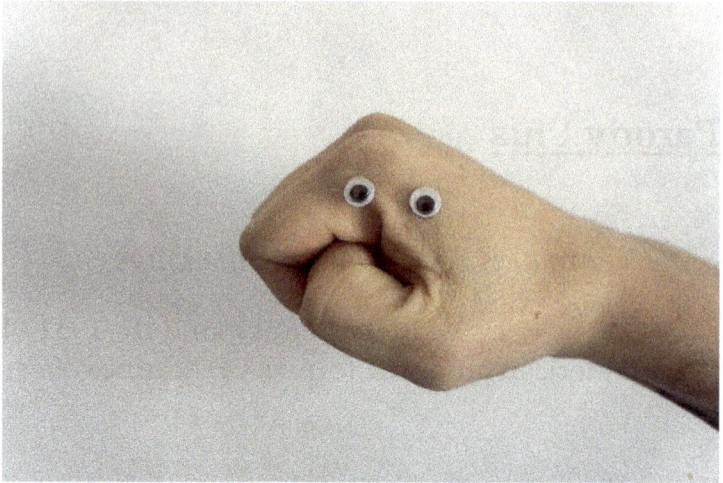

(Photo by Franco Antonio)

American comedy musician Alfred Matthew "Weird Al" Yankovic often performed comedy songs that parodied songs by contemporary musicians. Other times he played polka medleys on his accordion.

"If smart people are parodying it, that's a sure sign that some less smart people are believing it."

-- David Levithan (1972 -)
American author

That surreal slant or burlesque treatment of comedy reflects parody in low-brow humor. High-brow humor gets its day, too. Think about satire, irony, and clever sarcasm.

> "A day without sunshine is like, you know, night."
>
> -- Steve Martin (1945 -)
> American comedian, actor, writer, producer & musician

Satire reigns as especially effective when critiquing or ridiculing people, industries, politics and government, or society as a whole. Playwrights in the ilk of the French master Molière excelled at this.

Their audiences howled with laughter as broad characters twinkled with delicious social and political criticism over highly sensitive or totally taboo topics. This happened during times that could have otherwise landed playwrights and performers in prison at the very least. Instead, these actors and playwrights could even get the subject of their humor laughing, often not realizing they were being mocked.

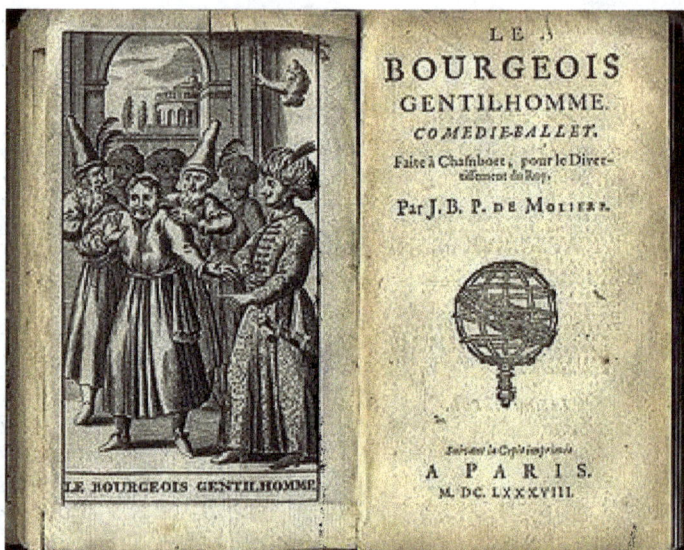

(1968 edition of Moliere's "Le Bourgeois Gentilhomme")

Irony and sarcasm also reign in favorite humor styles. Don Rickles again comes to mind as his routines regularly found him highlighting unflattering characterizations. He could be lighthearted and gentle, or he could come across as devilish or even cruel.

An entire era of comedy evolved in the form of roasts. "The Dean Martin Celebrity Roasts" became infamous. Hollywood celebrities lined the always star-studded table roasting one person in each event, ranging from Bob Hope, Wilt Chamberlain, and Hugh Hefner to then Governor Ronald Reagan, Zsa Zsa Gabor, and Joe Namath. Raucous humor filled the air, with seemingly no boundaries. Nearly every joke was targeted at the honoree.

Comedians often say the opposite of what is meant to create a humorous or critical effect. They can also sarcastically use caustic words, often in humorous ways to mock someone or something.

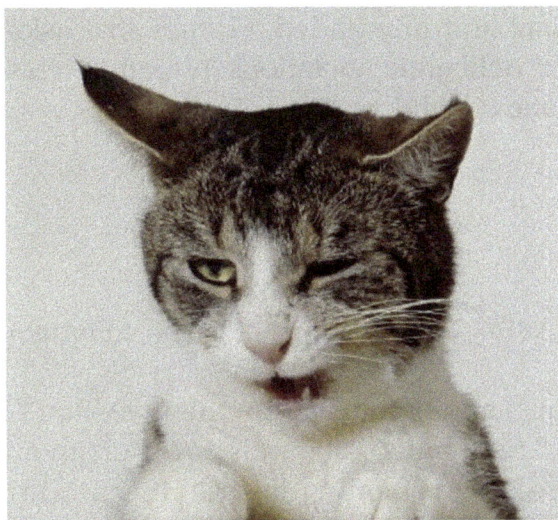

(Photo by Getty Images)

It's also fun to look at surreal humor or absurdity. Think about the British comedy series, "Monty Python's Flying Circus," launched in 1969. Their comedy sketches stretched from obscure to absolute absurdity as they explored strange situations and illogical events.

"There's no point in growing up
if you can't be childish sometimes."

-- Monty Python's Flying Circus

Surreal humor can be super silly with nonsensical themes, or it can defy expectations while playing with events and behaviors that are obviously irrational and unfounded. Humor that asks us to ponder deliberate violations of causal reasoning can make us think or laugh out loud.

"This is an argument."

"No, it isn't."

-- Monty Python's Flying Circus

A great example comes from the 1990 film, "Home Alone." Silly humor abounds based on an unlikely premise, as a family departs for a Christmas vacation and accidentally leaves their precocious young son home alone.

"If you're too busy to laugh,
you are too busy."
— Proverb

"I installed a skylight in my apartment… the
people who live above me are furious."

-- Steven Wright (1955 -)
American stand-up comedian, actor,
writer & producer

"I'd rather regret the things I've done than regret the things I haven't done."

– Lucille Ball (1911 – 1989)
American actress, comedian,
producer & studio executive

LIVE **FULLY**
CREATE **HAPPINESS**
SPEAK **KINDLY**
HUG **DAILY**
SMILE **OFTEN**
HOPE **MORE**
LAUGH **FREELY**
SEEK **TRUTH**
INSPIRE **CHANGE**
LIVE **DEEPLY**

(Photo by Ty Williams)

8

<u>Comedic Style</u>

I love watching great comedians at work. My favorites have had me laughing out loud right away and also laughing so hard at times that tears ran down my face.

Once we saw Rob Bartlet in a live theatre gig. Our stomachs literally ached from constant laughter from his "bits." For days afterward, we only had to say one word from any of his routines, and we'd all burst out laughing… again and again.

(Photo by E. Hillsley)

Those are rare moments. And yet, we were fortunate to meet a marvelous husband and wife comedic team in 2025. Kerri Louise opened, and she had me laughing hysterically with tears rushing down my cheeks.

Then she introduced her husband. Tom Cotter's bits flew so fast and furiously that laughter seemed to never stop in the theatre. It's no wonder that they bill themselves as "two comedians, one marriage, and a whole lot of funny."

Great stand-up comedians tend to emanate genuinely relatable personalities. They ooze with confidence, relaxation, and natural authenticity. Of course, on the inside, they may well be nervously hoping that everything goes as planned and that they score a hit with that event. I call this getting the butterflies in your stomach flying in formation.

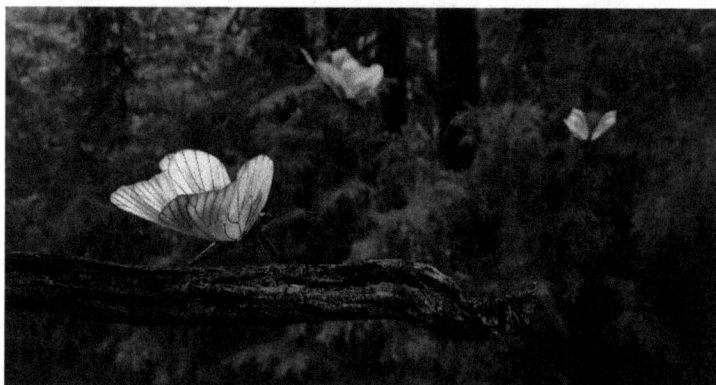

(Photo by Maria Shalabaieva)

Comic greats like Chris Rock, Robin Williams, and Sarah Silverman directly addressed their audiences with stories, one-liners, observations, and comic schtick. Stand-up comedians can also include props, magic, music, puppets, and ventriloquism.

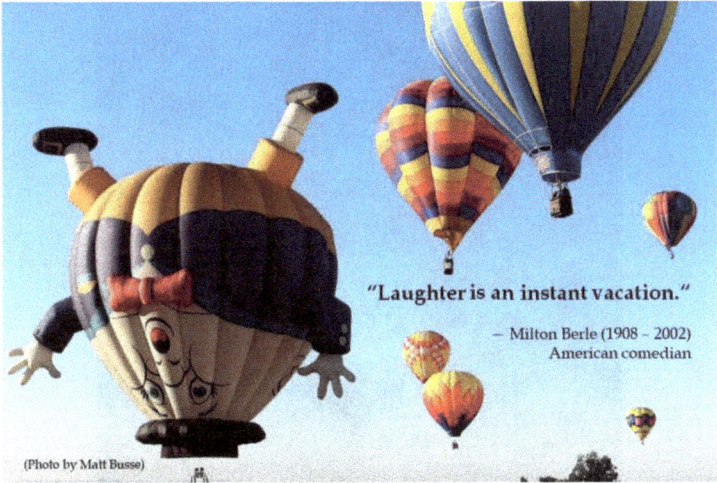

"Laughter is an instant vacation."

– Milton Berle (1908 – 2002)
American comedian

(Photo by Matt Busse)

"My sister was with two men in one night…
She could hardly walk after that.
Can you imagine?
Two dinners? That's a lot of food."

-- Sarah Silverman (1970 -)
American stand-up comedian, actress & writer

Peabody-winning American ventriloquist and puppeteer Shari Lewis comes to mind. Her "Lamb Chops" sock puppet remains a favorite of mine. "The Muppets," created by Jim Henson, forged an empire around comic puppetry.

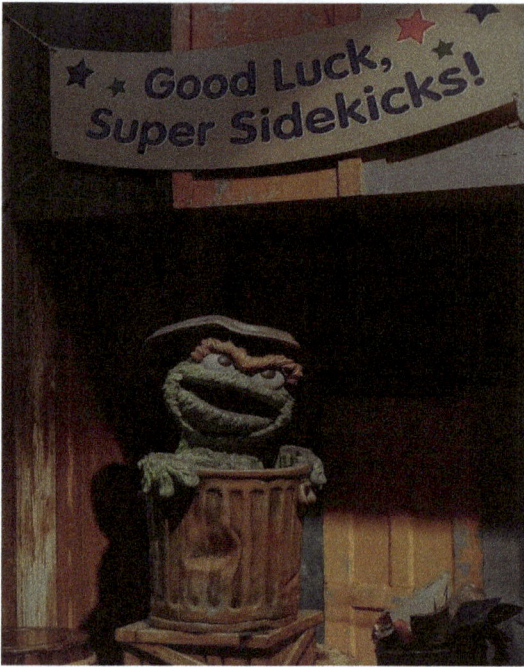

(Photo by Roynaldi Fredyn)

"My hope is to leave the world a bit better than when I got here."

-- Jim Henson (1936 – 1990)
American puppeteer, animator & director

We saw Ronn Lucas in Las Vegas. His skills as a ventriloquist and comedian kept us laughing for weeks. From his "Buffalo Billy" to that bad boy "Scorch," nonstop laughter could have been his calling card. Even years later, we would mimic a line from one of his bits and we'd laugh again. Humor doesn't get much better than that.

For me, at the top of the ventriloquist comedian ladder is Jeff Dunham. He creates a cast of characters that are stunningly hysterical, enabling him to deal with even the most sensitive, politically incorrect topics through comedy. His "Achmed, the Dead Terrorist" is a smashing example.

(Photo from Creative Artists Agency)

"It's amazing how these little guys can say things that a mortal human could never get away with. There's some sort of unspoken license... when outlandish things come out of an inanimate object, somehow it equals humor."

-- Jeff Dunham (1962 -)
American ventriloquist & stand-up comedian

We met a juggling comic on a cruise ship twenty years ago. He cleverly utilized his own name in his routine, loudly emphasizing his first name and saying it aloud along with his last name whenever he made a (likely deliberate) mistake in his juggling.

His name was DAN Bennet. Go ahead. Say it out loud. No, I mean frustratedly loud. Yup. It is like comic swearing. We laughed. And we never have forgotten his name.

Perfect pacing is paramount in comedic timing. Then, naturally, they work with body language and facial expressions. Their stories or bits must appear to be almost random. In truth, comedians hone their crafts constantly.

Practical but refined, each comedian hopes to create a memorable "brand" that is all their own. Through this they build a fan base. Rodney Dangerfield mastered this with his one-liners. These jokes and clever witticisms are often just one sentence long.

"When I was a kid my parents moved a lot, but I always found them."

-- Rodney Dangerfield (1921 - 2004)
American stand-up comedian & actor

Great comedy demands amazing creativity. Comedians must appear fresh, constantly adding elements of surprise.

"I saw what I saw when I saw it!"

-- Lou Costello (1906 – 1959)
American comedian, actor & producer

(Photo by Andre Mouton)

Great timing and double takes. Comedic teams Laurel and Hardy along with Abbot and Costello made careers that boosted the double take into the mainstream of future comedians. Jim Carrey and Gene Wilder are also noted by exaggerated facial expressions incorporating the classic double take.

"I was a milksop as a kid.
I had no confidence, no guts.
I felt I was going to be someone else someday -
someone who didn't have my weaknesses."

-- Gene Wilder (1933 – 2016)
American actor, comedian, writer & filmmaker

On the other hand, comedic style can lean toward the dark side of comedy. American comedian and actor Richard Pryor excelled at this.

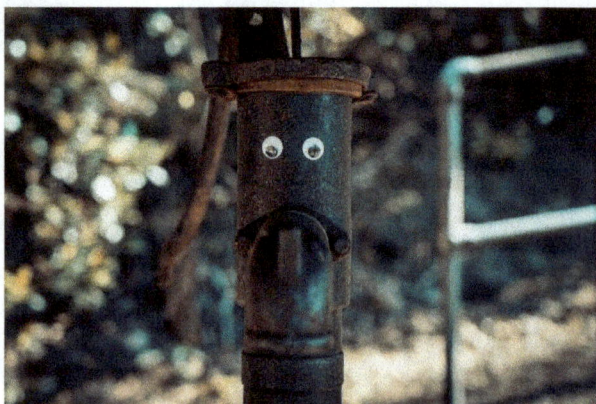

(Photo by Caleb Gios)

Dark humor pushes boundaries by tackling sensitive, taboo, or morbid topics in humorous or ironic ways. I often think of the edginess of George Carlin, who could make fun of otherwise serious situations.

> *"When fascism comes to America,*
> *it will not be in brown and black shirts.*
> *It will not be with jack-boots.*
> *It will be Nike sneakers and Smiley shirts."*
>
> -- George Carlin (1937 – 2008)
> American stand-up comedian, social critic,
> actor & author

Some broad comedy has also woven darkness into its fibers. The 1965 comedy "Hogan's Heroes" filled six seasons with various characters set in a prisoner of war camp. They regularly tackled serious subjects of death and war with light or satirized spins.

Consider New York shock jock Howard Stern who made a living out of making offensive, controversial, or outrageous comments. Radio legend Don Imus was fired for making derogatory comments that were notably over the top.

Shock comedy is pure low-brow, dark human. It is often used on the radio and features foul language, overt sexual themes, a mockery of serious subjects, and often tactless comments in the aftermath of a crisis. Shock humor is more than risqué, which can also offend some audience members.

(Photo by Earl Wilcox)

Being intentionally offensive was the fully committed style of Don Rickles. From Las Vegas to chumming with Frank Sinatra and the Rat Pack, Rickles' insult comedy frequently landed him on The Dean Martin Show, The Tonight Show Starring Johnny Carson, and the Late Show with David Letterman. Rickles was noted for lobbing insults at as many people in an audience as he possibly could.

"I wouldn't insult you,
but then again,
you're not bright enough to notice."

-- Don Rickles (1926 – 2017)
American stand-up comedian & actor

Of course, *self*-deprecating humor is always more pleasant, especially to anyone who has been on the receiving end of humor at our personal expense. When we poke fun at ourselves, we make ourselves the butt of jokes. Clever comedians specialize in highlighting their own flaws and gaffes in lighthearted ways.

"I once made love
for an hour and fifteen minutes,
but it was the night the clocks are set ahead."

-- Garry Shandling (1949 – 2016)
American comedian, writer & director

Pros at this comedic style include the likes of Don Knotts and Joan Rivers. They wore wide grins as they belittled, undervalued, and disparaged themselves.

*"I am definitely going to watch
the Emmys this year!
My makeup team is nominated for
Best Special Effects."*

-- Joan Rivers (1933 – 2014)
American comedian, actress, producer & writer

There is also self-enhancing humor. This style finds humor in hardships. It's not easy to stay positive in difficult situations. We can all benefit when we are able to use humor to manage harsh realities.

Smiling wryly at life's absurdities does not mean we are not taking life seriously. Rather, we are learning to survive turmoil in the healthiest way possible.

*"No man can be a genius
in slap shoes and a flat hat."*

-- Buster Keaton (1895 – 1966)
American actor, comedian,
director & producer

(Photo by David Clode)

Dry or deadpan humor has long been a successful staple in comedy. Known for his work in silent films, Buster Keaton excelled at stoicism to the point where he earned the nickname "The Great Stone Face."

"Everywhere is within walking distance… if you have the time."

-- Steven Wright (1955 -)
American stand-up comedian, actor,
writer & producer

Master of the one-liners, we love the lethargic style of American stand-up comedian Steven Wright. He is rightfully renowned for his nonsensical jokes, paraprosdokians, and one-liners with contrived situations.

A deadpan delivery style is intentionally flat and emotionless. The style is meant to be blunt, ironic, and expressing deliberate emotional neutrality. Great deadpan style catches an audience off guard and adds greatly to humor as it contrasts with the ridiculousness of the subject matter.

"A lot of people are afraid of heights. Not me. I'm afraid of widths."

-- Steven Wright (1955 -)
American stand-up comedian, actor, writer & producer

(Photo by Mark Basarab)

Some comedians use silly and colorful characters splendidly. American comedian Steve Martin created his "wild and crazy guy" on the renowned "Saturday Night Live" stage. Anyone who caught his stand-up routines likely recalls his "arrow through the head" headpiece.

"Before you criticize a man,
walk a mile in his shoes.
That way, when you do criticize him,
you'll be a mile away and have his shoes."

-- Steve Martin (1945 -)
American comedian, actor, writer,
producer & musician

(Photo by Dia Dipasupil / Getty Images)

When I think of characters created by comedians, my mind also flashes to the legendary American entertainer, Red Skelton. I love how he would laugh delightfully at himself.

I recall becoming enthralled with his seagull skits. He would tuck his hands up into his armpits and flap his elbows for wings. His seagull characters Gertrude and Heathcliff made me roar!

The two seagulls are flying, and Gertrude says, *"Look! Down there is a ship of fools."*

Heathcliff asks, *"How do you know they're a ship of fools?"*

Gertrude answers, *"They're looking up."*

(Photo from World Clown Association)

Of course, comedians who create these characters are not to be confused with comedians who do caricatures. These are the impressionists.

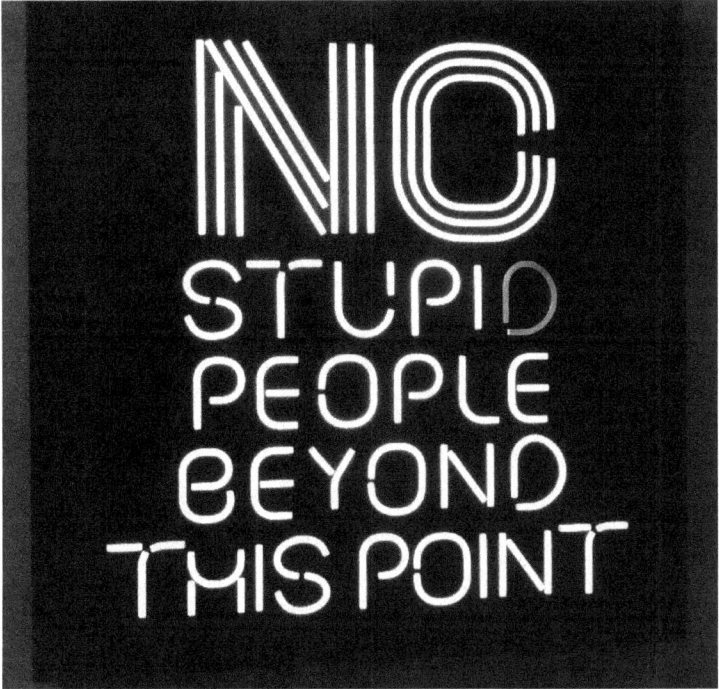

(Photo by Nick Fewings)

These impressions imitate sounds, voices and mannerisms of celebrities and politicians by delivering a distorted exaggeration (or sometimes highly precise depiction) of an actual person's characteristics or behavior.

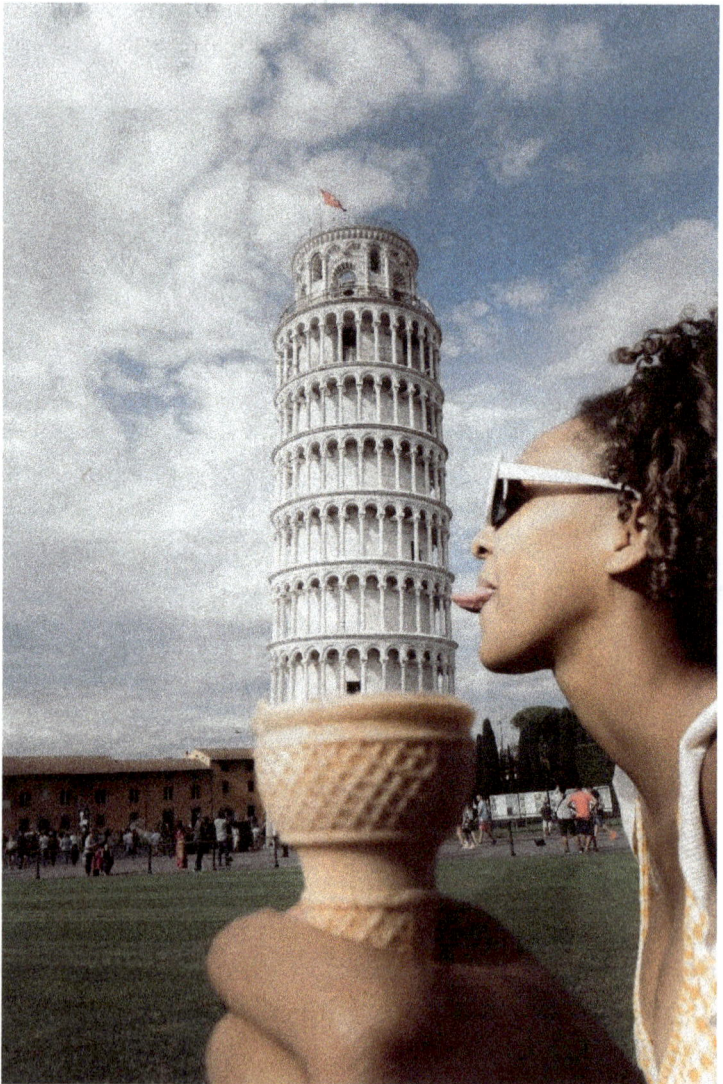

(Photo by Jakob Owens)

9

Genre Games

Comedy is a genre of dramatic works, designed to be humorous or amusing… definitely meant to induce laughter. Generally, we can count on happy endings.

As a literary genre, we see branches of theatre, cinema, stand-up, and broadcasting. As with all good humor, it entertains us with intrigues, errors, sentiments, and wonderful witticisms.

(Photo from Getty Images)

Often the sharpest writers of TV series turn dramas into "dramadies" by including lightness and humor... either straight forward or tongue-in-cheek. The dramady features elements of both comedy and drama.

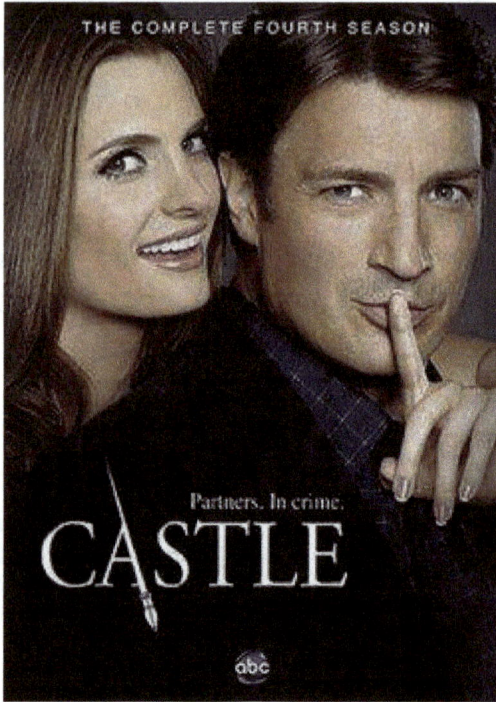

(Season 4 DVD cover; ABC)

"Castle," starring Nathan Fillion and a tremendous cast, still reigns as my favorite. Many other series work for that delicate mix of comedy in a drama. Series that worked successfully to capture that special emotional authenticity include "Suits," "Orange Is the New Black," "Gilmore Girls," and "Parenthood."

Another slice of comedy comes from the theatre and the musical theatre pie. On stage or screen, we enjoy theatrical humor. Characters triumph over negative circumstances, while combining elements like music, acting, conversation, dancing, and singing. Plays and movies such as "My Fair Lady" and "Grease" quickly come to mind.

1964 album cover

Not all musical humor is locked into romantic comedy. Some musical comedy bits are simply geared toward having fun with music.

I recall being at a theatre opening night cast party for "West Side Story," in which I had appeared with a young Adam Sandler. As usual, he picked up his guitar and started crafting some hysterical rewrites of songs from the show, beginning with the character Maria's "I Feel Pretty."

Later, Sandler launched his phenomenally successful, professional comedic career, writing and performing humorous musical bits for "Saturday Night Live." Not many other humorists can deftly weave places like New Hampshire's Lake Winnipesaukee into their lyrics.

The humorous sketch plays a lead role in comedy. A sketch is typically a series of short, amusing scenes, from 1 to 10 minutes in length. Sketches feature a group of comic actors or comedians playing all sorts of funny characters. "Saturday Night Live" has many dozens of classic sketches. For me, the queen of comic sketches was Carol Burnett.

(Carol Burnett photo from The Hollywood Reporter)

Sketches are different from sit-coms. The situational comedy features the same characters typically carrying over from episode to episode. While there is a plethora of sit-coms available, I think they all would like to capture the fame and success of the likes of "I Love Lucy," "Cheers," or "All in the Family."

(Marx Brothers photo from The New Yorker)

Improvisational humor is a delightful part of this genre, too. The Marx Brothers, and Second City are noted for this form of theatre, which is often especially humorous.

I think of it as comedy without a plan. Sketches are unplanned, unscripted, and created spontaneously.

We often see improvisations by street artists of all sorts. They range from comedians and clowns to musicians.

(Photo by Peter Pryharski)

10

In Closing

Humor has undergone numerous ch-ch-ch-changes as the decades and centuries pass. We humans have always loved to laugh.

(Photo by Lachlan Gowen)

However, in recent years, a challenge has arisen. We seem to have become super sensitive to humor, causing comedy to be negatively polarizing.

We tend to take things far too personally. In doing so, we don't always let ourselves see the humorous side of things.

Polarization particularly peaked over politics. We like whatever we believe to be true and factual and prefer to see other thoughts and viewpoints as negative, unworthy, or even evil. We humans have become distinctly unfun.

*"Whenever you find yourself
on the side of the majority,
it is time to pause and reflect."*

-- Mark Twain (1835 – 1910)
American writer & humorist

Many people adapted and learned to self-censor to avoid potentially offending someone. It takes great personal courage to not let the "Cancel Culture" squelch our ability to laugh, especially at our most assuredly silly selves.

We all benefit when we stop taking ourselves so seriously. Or, as Mom taught me, "Always take what you *do* seriously, but not your*self*."

> *"I bought a sail for my boat*
> *on Amazon the other day.*
> *Today it dawned on me*
> *that it's not the right size,*
> *so I called to cancel.*
> *They said, 'It's too late.*
> *That sail has shipped.'"*

With humor we can discover, express, or appreciate the ludicrous or absurdly incongruous. Good humor makes us better humans and infinitely more relatable. (This does not include Don Rickles' styled put downs.)

Watch an episode of "The Dean Martin Celebrity Roast." These ran for 10 seasons starting in 1974. We still had a collective sense of humor then. Today? I do not think even one episode would survive the scrutiny of our raging Cancel Culture.

"It may feel good to think you're right.
But it's better to allow
the possibility that you're wrong."

-- Greg Gutfeld (1964 -)
American TV host, political commentator,
comedian & author

(Photo by Gary Bendig)

"Postwar America
was a very buttoned up nation.
Radio shows were run by censors,
Presidents wore hats, ladies wore girdles.
We came straight out of the blue –
nobody was expecting anything like
Martin and Lewis.
A sexy guy and a monkey –
that's how some people saw us."

-- Jerry Lewis (1926 – 2017)
American comedian, actor & humanitarian

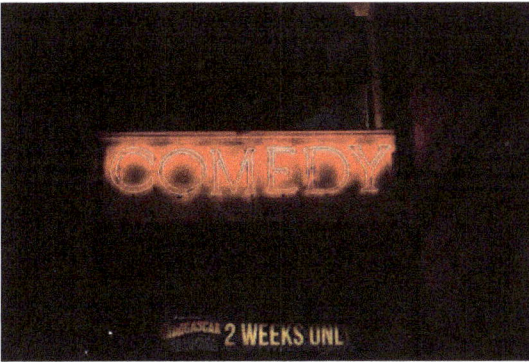

"No matter what people tell you, words and
ideas can change the world."

-- Robin Williams (1951 – 2014)
American comedian & actor

--- --- --- --- ---

If you would like to know when new editions in
the *Life Seasonings* series
or any other titles are released,
along with any other formats such as audiobooks,
follow
Cathy Burnham Martin
on Facebook or frequent her
www.GoodLiving123.com site.

(Photo by Joe Caione)

Photography Credits

Thank you to everyone who entrusted me with the use of their beautiful photographs.

Denis Agati
Diane Alkier
Braydon Anderson
Christo Anestev
Franco Antonio
Simon Arthur
Hussain Badshah
Mark Basarab
Gary Bendig
Matt Busse
Ashley Byrd
Joe Caione
David Clode
Uwe Conrad
Dan Cook
Creative Artists Agency
Charles DeLuvio
Shubham Dhage
Dia Dipasupil
Fabian Fauth
Nick Fewings
Roynaldi Fredyn
Getty Images
Caleb Gios

Lachlan Gowen
Michel Grolet
E. Hillsley
Kateryna Hliznitsova
The Hollywood Reporter
The New Yorker
Jamie Haughton
Mikael Kristenson
Library of Congress
Looney Tunes Wiki Fandom
Jarnie Matocinos
Andre Mouton
Jakob Owens
Chaitanya Pillala
Peter Pryharski
Victoria Romulo
San Diego Oasis
Maria Shalabaieva
Thapanee Srisawa
Frank Tokluoglu
Leo Visions
Earl Wilcox
Ty Williams
World Clown Assn.

Special thanks to Nathan Anderson
for the cover photo.

(Cover photo by Nathan Anderson)

About the Author

Cathy Burnham Martin's first published work came in elementary school when an early poem won a town library contest. That was back when her parents refused to let her have the then-popular "Chatty Cathy" doll, stating that one chatty Cathy in the house was more than enough. Though poetry took a back seat, she drove her writing and blabbing proficiencies along a highly eclectic career path through college recruitment, telecom marketing, corporate communications, TV broadcasting with an ABC affiliate, station management of an award-winning PEG-access station, bank organizing, and investor relations. An active board member and volunteer, she received Easter Seals' David P. Goodwin Lifetime Commitment Award. This professional voiceover artist, humorist, musical actress, journalist, and dedicated foodie earned numerous awards as a news anchor and businesswoman. She has produced and hosted groundbreaking documentaries, TV specials, and news reports, from the Moscow Superpower Summit and the opening of the Berlin Wall to coverage of Presidential Primaries. A born storyteller and business speaker dubbed "The Morale Booster," Cathy is a member of Actors Equity and writes daily articles for social media and the GoodLiving123.com website.

"*People will pay more to be entertained than educated.*"

-- Johnny Carson (1925 – 2005)
American comedian, writer &
television host

(Photo by Uwe Conrad)

Other Titles

Life Seasonings series:
   Perspectives   Happiness
   Hope   Forgiveness

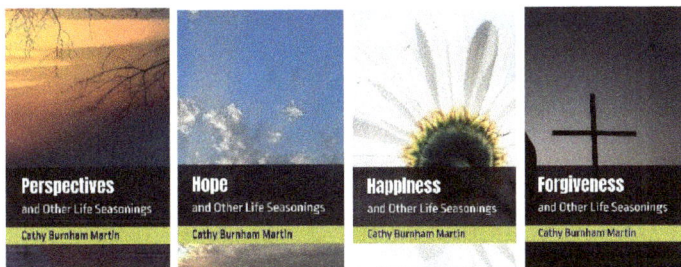

The Destiny trilogy:
   Destiny of Dreams… Time Is Dear
   Destiny of Determination… Faith and Family
   Destiny of Daring… Never Forget

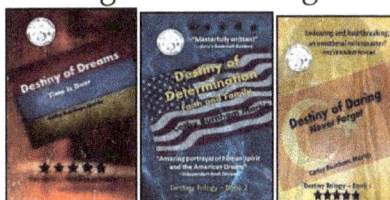

A Dangerous Book for Dogs:
     Train Your Humans with the Bandit Method
Dog Days in the Life of the Miles-Mannered Man

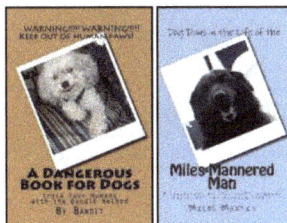

Healthy Thinking Habits:
    Seven Attitude Skills Simplified
Good Living Skills: Learned from My Mother
Encouragement: How to Be and Find Your Best

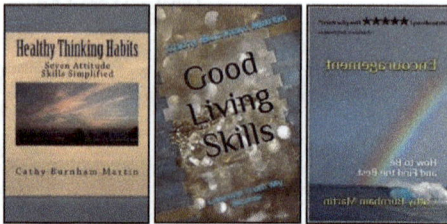

Of the Same Blood: Your Eurasian Heritage
The Ronald…
    Daydreams, Wonderments & Other Ponderings

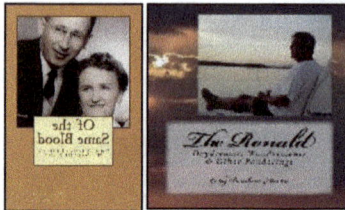

The Bimbo Has Brains… and Other Freaky Facts
The Bimbo Has MORE Brains…
    Surviving Political Correctness

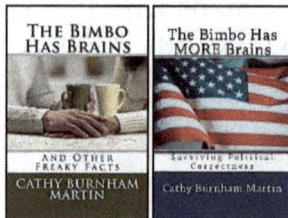

From the KISS Keep It Super Simple cookbooks:

50 Years of Fabulous Family Favorites
   Sippers, Starters, and Sweets
   Lunch, Brunch, and Entrees
   Sides, Soup, Salad, Snacks, Etc.

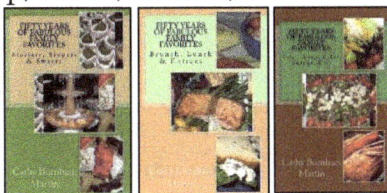

Champagne! Facts, Fizz, Food, & Fun
Cranberry Cooking

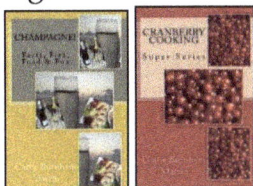

Dockside Dining: (series)
   Round One
   A Second Helping
   Back for Thirds

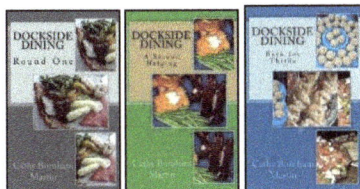

Lobacious Lobster…
 Decadently Super Simple Recipes

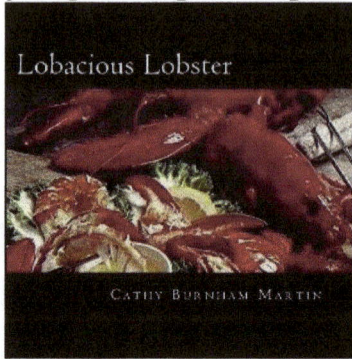

Find all books by Cathy Burnham Martin in paperback, digital, and audiobook formats anywhere books are sold and on her **www.GoodLiving123.com** site.

Partial List of Audiobooks Narrated by Cathy Burnham Martin

Fiction

Destiny Trilogy:

Destiny of Dreams... Time Is Dear
(Violent content warning)

Destiny of Determination... Faith and Family

Destiny of Daring... Never Forget

A Dangerous Book for Dogs...

Train Your Humans with the Bandit Method

Kremlins Trilogy (Violent content warning)

Citadels of Fire

Bastions of Blood

Dungeons of Destiny:

An Epic Russian Historical Romance

Daniel's Fork: A Mystery Set in the

Daniel's Fork Universe

(Adult content warning)

The Relentless Brit

Non-Fiction

Encouragement: How to Be and Find the Best

Good Living Skills... Learned from My Mother

Healthy Thinking Habits:

Seven Attitude Skills Simplified

The Bimbo Has Brains: And Other Freaky Facts

The Bimbo Has MORE Brains:

Surviving Political Correctness

31 Days to a Stronger Marriage:

A Guide to Building Closer Relationships

Exploring Past Lives: A Guide to the Soul's Travels

Why We Fail in Love: A Study into the Pursuit of

One of Mankind's Most Precious Desires

The Hormone Fix: Naturally Rebalance Your System
in 10 Weeks